★
THE
BIG
TIME

KATY
PERRY

AARON FRISCH

CREATIVE  EDUCATION

KATY PERRY

TABLE OF CONTENTS

MEET KATY

The *arena* is dark. Fireworks go off, and loud music starts. The crowd cheers as Katy walks onto the stage. Colored lights shine on her blue hair and pink dress. Katy smiles and begins to sing.

Katy Perry (whose real name is Katheryn Hudson) is one of the biggest pop stars today. Her hit songs play on the radio all the time. And with Katy's colorful *fashion*, her concerts are exciting to both hear and see.

Katy wears colorful and unusual outfits to her shows and events

KATY'S CHILDHOOD

Katy was born October 25, 1984, in Santa Barbara, California. Her parents were *pastors*, and Katy was allowed to listen only to **Christian music**. When she was nine, she started singing in a church choir.

Katy with her grandmother, Ann, before the 2011 Grammy Awards

SANTA BARBARA, CALIFORNIA

GETTING INTO MUSIC

K aty graduated from high school when she was only 15. She decided she wanted to be a musical performer. She went to Nashville, Tennessee, to learn about writing and recording music.

Katy decided early on that music was going to be her life

NASHVILLE, TENNESSEE

In 2001, Katy released an album that was partly Christian and partly rock. Not many people bought the album. She then recorded different kinds of music. In 2007, she began calling herself Katy Perry.

Katy in 2007 (right) and performing a pop concert in 2010 (left)

THE BIG TIME

In 2008, Katy recorded an album called *One of the Boys*. It had songs like "Hot N Cold" on it. Fans liked the music, and they liked Katy's concerts, too. In 2009, she went on *tour* around the world.

In 2009, Katy did many concerts in America, Europe, Japan, and Australia

By 2010, Katy was a huge star. People bought more than 2 million copies of her next album, *Teenage Dream*. In 2011, MTV gave her an award for Artist of the Year.

Katy thanked her fans when she accepted the MTV Artist of the Year Award

OFF THE STAGE

When she is not performing, Katy likes to shop. She likes to act, too. In 2011, she did a voice for the cartoon movie *The Smurfs*. Katy got married in 2010, but she and her husband divorced a year later.

Smurfette (right) had Katy's voice

WHAT IS NEXT?

Besides singing and acting, Katy helps create her own perfumes. In 2012, Katy starred in a movie called *Part of Me*. She began working on a new album, too. Katy plans to entertain her fans for many more years!

Katy's perfumes "Purr" and "Meow!" come in cat-shaped bottles

WHAT KATY SAYS ABOUT ...

HER FAVORITE FOODS

"I ... crave Chicken McNuggets and bacon, which is the meat candy of the world."

SINGING AS A KID

"My dad would give me $10 ... to sing at church, on tables at restaurants, at family functions, just about anywhere."

WRITING SONGS

"Everything I write, whether it's happy or sad, has a sense of humor to it."

GLOSSARY

arena a large building with many seats that holds sports events or concerts

Christian music music that is about God or religious subjects

fashion a certain style or way of dressing

pastors religious leaders in a church

tour a series of concerts in different cities within a country or around the world

READ MORE

Adams, Michelle Medlock. *Katy Perry*. Hockessin, Del.: Mitchell Lane, 2001.

Tieck, Sarah. *Katy Perry: Singing Sensation*. Minneapolis: Abdo, 2011.

WEB SITES

Katy Perry
http://wwwkatyperry.com/home/
This is Katy's own Web site, with news and videos.

Katy Perry Biography
http://www.people.com/people/katy_perry/
This site has information about Katy's life and many pictures, too.

INDEX

PUBLISHED BY Creative Education
P.O. Box 227, Mankato, Minnesota 56002
Creative Education is an imprint of The Creative Company
www.thecreativecompany.us

DESIGN AND PRODUCTION BY Christine Vanderbeek
ART DIRECTION BY Rita Marshall
PRINTED IN the United States of America

PHOTOGRAPHS BY Alamy (International Artists, Photos 12), Dreamstime (Kody Little), Getty Images (Jeff Kravitz/FilmMagic, George Pimentel/WireImage, Matthew Simmons/WireImage, Gus Stewart/Redferns, Chris Wolf/FilmMagic), iStockphoto (Pingebat, Cole Vineyard), Shutterstock (Helga Esteb, Harmony Gerber, Anton Oparin, s_bukley, Debby Wong)

LIBRARY OF CONGRESS CATALOGING-IN-PUBLICATION DATA
Frisch, Aaron.
Katy Perry / Aaron Frisch.
p. cm. — (The big time)
Includes bibliographical references and index.
Summary: An elementary introduction to the life, work, and popularity of Katy Perry, an American pop singer known for her colorful stage performances and such hit songs as "Hot N Cold."

ISBN 978-1-60818-331-9
1. Perry, Katy—Juvenile literature. 2. Singers—United States—Biography—Juvenile literature. I. Title.
ML3930.P455F75 2013
782.42164092—dc23 [B]   2012013470

First edition
9 8 7 6 5 4 3 2 1